A Woman's

Shirley Baxter and Jean Lees

Sheffield General Cemetery Trust

Acknowledgements

This project was funded entirely by the Heritage Lottery Fund Parks for People project and administered through Sheffield City Council. The Sheffield General Cemetery Trust gratefully acknowledges the Sheffield City Council Archive, and the Local Studies service for their ongoing support. The authors would also like to thank all those at the Trust who contributed their time and expertise, and also, historian David Boursnall and the family of Alice Hall for their help.

'A Woman's Place' is a revised and expanded edition of 'She Lived Unknown' by Jools Duggleby and Jean Lees, originally researched by The Friends of the General Cemetery and revised in 2013 by Nancy Greenwood, Jo Pye and Jo Meredith. Several entries in "A Woman's Place" can be found on the SGCT website. Others have previously been published in "Undertakings", the Cemetery magazine.

Additional research by: Sue Turner, Hilary McAra, Cathy Spence (SGCT research volunteers), David Boursnall and Laura Alston.

Burial research is ongoing. The facts as presented in this book were correct at the time of publication.

Printed by Mensa Printers 323 Abbeydale Road, Sheffield, S7 1F

Published by the Sheffield General Cemetery Trust 2023

"She looketh well to the ways of her household and eateth not the bread of idleness."

Proverbs 31 v.27

Inscription on Jemima Binns' memorial.

Contents

Introduction   7

Symbolism in the Cemetery   13

Women in Poverty   18

Women and Childbirth   29

Women in Business   33

Self-supporting Women   42

Women in the Arts   51

Politically Engaged Women   55

Women and Medicine   60

Women of Means   65

Index of Names   78

Further Reading   82

Please note there are references to sensitive subjects such as suicide and infant death. Additionally, there may be some terminology cited that was used at the time which is considered offensive and outdated today. This book will quote some of these terms where relevant. When not quoting directly from historical sources, modern terminology will be used.

SHEFFIELD GENERAL CEMETERY

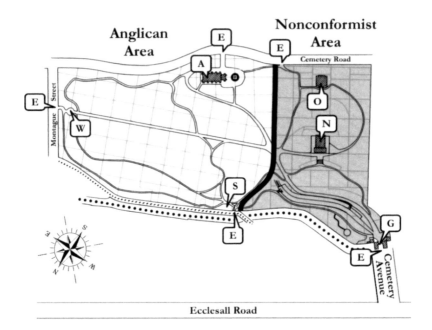

Dissenters' Wall

A Anglican Chapel

N Nonconformist Chapel
(Samuel Worth Chapel)

G Gatehouse

O Old Cemetery Office

////// Stalker Walk

•••• Porter Brook

E Entrance

W War Memorial

S Stone Spiral

Introduction

The Cemetery's burial records give details of everyone in the cemetery - name, age, date of death, date of burial, address, and, in the case of men, occupation. Women are only ever recorded in terms of their marital status - as wives, widows, or spinsters - even if they had a role outside the home. Alice Hall, children's author, tireless worker for women's causes and a J.P., who died as late as 1935, is simply recorded in the burial register as "widow" and on the family grave as a "beloved wife." Some women, such as Catherine Parker, widowed at the time of her death, were referred to in their memorial inscriptions as "relict of", meaning "widow". Men in public life were referred to in local newspapers whenever they were engaged in anything of note, and when they died, they were frequently given a detailed obituary. Women were largely invisible in this respect: for most of the nineteenth century their lives were not reported in the newspapers, except perhaps for brief marriage and death notices, unless they died in less than respectable circumstances. Not until the turn of the century did this begin to change, but even then, for a woman to be awarded an obituary was a rare event.

It is sometimes possible to glimpse hints of the lives of some nineteenth century women from occasional, almost accidental details. While census records give the name of women, their ages, marital status and place of birth, no occupation was generally recorded for a middle-class married woman, who was expected to be at home, busy with domestic duties. Single adult middle-class women would also be listed as "at home", although towards the end of the century if they had a profession such as teaching, that might be recorded. Adult daughters of a working-class man were more frequently recorded as having an occupation, but there is less information on the wives and mothers. Yet the image of the

Victorian "angel of the house", creating a stress-free haven for the men returning home from the outside world was a middle-class ideal rather than a working-class reality. Women, and indeed children, needed to work to support their families, particularly when a woman was widowed, but employment opportunities were limited, lacking in permanence, and badly paid. For unmarried women domestic service was almost the only option, although they could also work as bonnet makers and dressmakers. Widows might let rooms, or set up as grocers, perhaps selling a few items from a room in their home. A few women ran businesses inherited from husbands but even then, tended to trade in their husband's name rather than their own. Only a very few women, widows such as Hannah and Mary Cadman or Charlotte Taylor, were described as manufacturers in their own right.

Among metal workers, daughters of cutlers were often involved in the finishing process. Whatever a man's speciality, when based at home, it was likely that the whole family would be helping, the children being brought up to follow him. The sons of a cutler might be listed as "cutler's apprentice", meaning that they were being trained by their father, but girls, who might well be picking up skills informally, were excluded by the Cutlers Company and so were often not recorded.

Literate middle-class women with money could leave more of a trace of their lives, particularly if they wrote letters or left a will. Others, like Nancy Senior, wife of a Master Cutler and Mayor, who lived until 1913, might be mentioned in newspaper accounts of their husbands' activities. Politically active women who fought for women's suffrage were also mentioned in newspaper reports, but it was not until the twentieth century that women became the subject of obituaries. The exceptions were women like Maria Gomersal and Jane Callender who, as performers, had already been the subject of show reviews.

Early death in all classes, but particularly in the working class, meant that many did not live long enough to be noticed by bureaucracy. Working men's wages could be unreliable and a job was something that you did when work was available. Industrialisation later in the nineteenth century meant that a family could separate at five in the morning to work 12 to 14 hour days at various factories. In these times of extreme social inequality, despite the hours of hard labour, there was grinding poverty, one of main factors which led to the premature deaths of women and children. Other factors such as overcrowded housing, ignorance about the causes of disease, and the lack and expense of effective medicines, were also closely related to poverty. It has been calculated that in the mid nineteenth century five mothers died for every thousand live births. However, this did not include deaths relating to miscarriage or stillbirth. Puerperal fever following childbirth increased in the second half of the nineteenth century, and deaths from the infection accounted for half of maternal mortality from 1885 to 1894.

Pregnancy outside marriage led to social stigma and economic disaster. Many women would conceal their pregnancies to keep their paid work. The stigma of illegitimacy also meant that some babies were abandoned, resulting in the tragic "baby no name" being recorded in the surname section of the burial record. On 4 June 1850 a newly born child was discovered drowned. On 1 July 1853 the body of a female baby was found naked and floating in the goit of a dam near the General Cemetery. On 6 April 1869 the body of a newly born boy was found in a drain, wrapped in paper. On 17 April 1878, the body of a female child was found in Old Park Wood. Poignantly, this child was "properly laid out" in a grocer's box and wearing an elaborate nightgown.

Even when an illegitimate baby was named, like Minnie Clarke's baby, Kenneth, their fate would be uncertain and their life chances precarious. At the very least poverty meant a poor diet, overcrowded housing, and ignorance about hygiene and the causes of disease. Although the new middle classes lived comfortably in the leafy districts of Ranmoor, Endcliffe, and Fulwood, the 1832 cholera epidemic in which 402 people died in Sheffield, also took the life of the Master Cutler John Blake, and was thought to have been caused by air born "miasmas". The overcrowding of churchyards with their offensive smells and the perceived public health dangers was a major factor in the minds of Sheffield's great and good who founded the General Cemetery Company. However, it wasn't until the 1875 Public Health Act, which forced local councils to provide clean water, proper drainage and sewage systems, along with a recognition that cholera was a water born disease, that there would be an improvement in the town's welfare.

Consumption, or tuberculosis, was also an ever-present danger, attacking all classes. Of the first three burials in the cemetery, two were of women who died of tuberculosis. This infectious disease which attacks the lungs was a common killer being quickly spread through overcrowded and insanitary housing but neither of these women lived in poverty. Mary Ann Fish, the first person to be buried in the Cemetery, was born in Hull in 1814 to William and Ann Tummon. William was a mariner and ship owner - a common occupation in Hull. Mary married James Fish, a bookkeeper, and died 23 May 1836, aged 24.

Mary Ann Whewell also succumbed to consumption. She was 29 and married to John Whewell, an ironmonger. Her address appears in the records as "Bradford", but she was born in Sheffield.

Her father, Thomas Sawyer, a porter dealer, owned the grave. She died on 18 June 1836 and was buried next to Mary Ann Fish. Jane Marshall, the third person to be interred, died in childbirth aged 25. We know little about her, except she was born in Sheffield, that her father, John Saylor, was a publican and that she was married to Christopher Marshall, who purchased the plot.

The life of an unmarried or widowed woman was often very harsh and could result in entry to the workhouse. There was very little other help. Sheffield's House of Help for Friendless Girls, formed to support vulnerable girls and women, was not founded until the last decade of the nineteenth century. It provided a temporary refuge and training for employment and was supported by women who lived in more affluent circumstances. The House of Help did not close its doors until 2005. Another charitable initiative, the Deakin Fund, was established in 1852, thanks to the legacy of businessman Thomas Deakin. Still in existence today, it aims to help single, divorced, or widowed women over forty years old who are in need or living in hardship, if they are active members of a church.

The workhouse was entered only as a last resort. The nearest workhouse to the General Cemetery was Ecclesall Bierlow Workhouse at Nether Edge, which has now been converted into luxury apartments. Those unfortunate enough to end their lives in the workhouse were buried in public graves, as were those who simply could not afford a private burial. The largest public grave holds 85 burials, the majority young children.

Grinding poverty destroyed the morale of many. Alcohol offered a temporary respite, and it is not surprising that drunkenness among the poor was an ongoing concern of those trying to improve social conditions. Sarah Grace and Elizabeth Neild are examples of women whose short, destitute and desperate lives ended as a result of excessive drinking and who were buried in public graves. Their deaths were reported by the local newspapers in disapproving tones. Women's drunkenness always seems to have been more harshly condemned than that of men.

This book tells the stories of some of the women buried in the General Cemetery and provides a general context of women's lives in the nineteenth and early twentieth centuries within a society organised by, and for, the interests of men. It can be argued that the condition of women was more desperate than that of men for this reason. Childbirth certainly took its toll; either a woman was worn out from frequently giving birth or she was mourning the deaths of some of those same babies. Depression, post-natal or otherwise, was rarely recognised. Some women, even the more privileged, were driven to desperate measures – rarely murder but more often suicide, as in the case of Catherine Parker, who despite having a financially comfortable life, was ultimately overwhelmed by the difficulties of managing responsibilities from the shadows.

The first three burials in the Cemetery were in the Nonconformist area, Section LL. Mary Ann Fish is in Plot 70, Mary Ann Whewell in Plot 71 and Jane Marshall in Plot 69. The three graves are no longer visible.

Symbolism in the Cemetery

The garden cemetery symbolises the wider social change in the nineteenth century. The cemetery as 'park' might be, as the *Sheffield Mercury* reported in 1836, 'a pleasant grassy lawn by the side of the river Porter', but it also reflected the contrast between the emerging middle classes and the poor: fine monuments and public graves. Ironically, it was revenue from workhouse burials in both the Anglican and Nonconformist areas which the Cemetery Company relied on as a core income. For the middle class, death became another aspect of consumer culture, and a fashion for all things Egyptian and classical, was an important influence on the design of the General Cemetery.

When we walk round the Cemetery and stop to examine individual graves, we might wonder about the meaning behind the often intricate and ornate plaques which decorate them and some of the larger figures. Symbolism played an important role in Victorian life, and the relative commissioning the stone would have wanted to ensure it reflected some aspect of the departed person's life as well as drawing attention to their own status in society. Carved stones were expensive. The Victorian taking a stroll round the Cemetery would have been able to understand the  significance of the symbols and their more intricate meanings. Such carvings are more often found embellishing graves in the

Anglican area whereas the Nonconformist graves are relatively austere, though some Nonconformist headstones favour urns on the top of monuments. The urn symbolises the death of the body but not the soul. In its reference to Greek and Roman culture, it would also signify a level of good taste and knowledge of prevailing fashions.

Many urns are covered with drapery representing the veil between life and death, as on the headstone on Hannah Martha Wilson's grave. Some carving is more expert than others. For example, the draped urn on Major Morton's monument seems very inexpertly rendered which is interesting because he was a sculptor of marble monuments and had made it himself. Drapery may also reflect contemporary death customs where household items like mirrors were covered.

Wreaths were another classical symbol adopted by the Victorians to represent victory over death. In ancient Greece, a wreath was presented to a winning Olympic athlete, while Roman generals who were triumphant in battle, were crowned with laurel or oak leaves. Mary Oates' headstone has a beautiful example of a wreath of laurel leaves. There also seems to be lily of the valley adorning the sides of the stone. Lilies of the valley represented a return of happiness after the expulsion of Eve from the garden of Eden. Eve's tears are said to have turned to lilies as they fell to the ground.

Angels were seen as agents of God and guardians of the dead. They guard the tomb, guide the soul, pray for the soul, and direct the living to think of heaven.

Although angels are often believed to be androgynous, the few angel statues which still exist in the Cemetery are clearly female, though relatively modest compared to those in some continental cemeteries who have shapely bodies and dresses clinging in a rather revealing way.

On the headstone which stands on Walter Beatson's grave, there is an angel with beautifully carved robes and magnificent wings. The angel is standing under a weeping tree, a symbol of human sadness, mourning and mortality. (See frontispiece).

William Hardcastle's headstone features a more pious angel with hands folded in prayer inside what is possibly a church window. This may reflect a transition between Victorian symbolism and a more conventional Anglican fashion as this 70 year old's death occurred in 1914. Figures of women symbolise grief, and there are also relief plaques on headstones showing women's heads bowed or their bodies slumped in grief. They are sometimes on graves dedicated to a woman but also on those of men.

On Thomas Brookes' grave, a plaque shows a weeping woman who kneels beside a tomb on which rests an urn. Thomas Binney's plaque has a weeping woman and an angel in profile who seems to have a hand raised in benediction.

The grieving woman with her head in her hands, shown on Charlotte Jinkinson's grave, is leaning on a tomb which bears the words 'to mother'.

One of the most striking monuments is the one dedicated to Harriet and James Nicholson. It shows a woman, perhaps kneeling in prayer, as she points up towards heaven with her right hand. Sadly, her pointing finger has long since broken off. There were originally four angels at each side of the plinth, but they were victims of thefts which the Cemetery suffered from in the 1980s. Only one small foot remains.

Generally, flowers reflect the frailty of life, and bouquets symbolise condolences and grief.

A garland of flowers is depicted in relief on a plaque dedicated to Sarah Elizabeth Gray. Most of the flowers seen on memorials are stylised and similar to each other rather than realistic, which suggests that they were from a pattern book. Sarah Gray's headstone has rose-like flowers which can symbolise love, with an open rose for a married woman and closed buds for a child or unmarried woman.

These images of women may seem to the modern gaze to be portrayed in submissive attitudes and would certainly have both reflected and reinforced the general Victorian attitudes towards 'angels in the house'. In this sense at least, we can interpret the General Cemetery's garden design as a setting in which a woman's place was defined as subservient to men.

Women in Poverty

Sarah Cheshire

Many working-class women, while not destitute, struggled with poverty and the difficulties of subsisting on a small, fluctuating income. When they died, those left behind often lacked the money for a private plot, and even the modest fees required for burial in a public grave could sometimes be a struggle to find.

Sarah Cheshire was one of the many working-class people who could not afford a private plot and so were buried in a public grave. She was one of nine people in the plot, six of them, like Sarah, buried in late 1884. The final three were added in 1892,1896 and 1899.

Sarah was born Sarah Ann Wild in 1817 to John Wild and his wife Julia. Within a year of her marriage to George Bailey she was a widow with a baby son. The 1841 Census records her as being a pen knife grinder and living in High field with her mother, brother William, and sister Hannah. George Junior died in infancy. A few years later she married Richard Cheshire with whom she had four children, James, Fanny, Sarah and John. An occupation was not given for Sarah in the 1851 Census, when they were living at seventh Court, Granville Terrace, although they had a lodger, Elizabeth Blagden, who was 22 and a file dresser. However, by 1861, she was once again a widow, this time with three daughters aged 11, 9 and 6, living at home. Sarah was now a file scourer, and she had two female lodgers, one of whom was a 17-year-old fileswoman. Ten years later Sarah was found lodging with her brother William, a spring knife grinder, and his family. Her daughter Fanny and a baby grandson were also listed as lodgers. It is not known what happened to Sarah and Fanny after William died the following year. She was living in Harvest Lane at the time of her death.

Of the others in the same plot, one was Harriet Hannah Joule Briggs, the four-year-old daughter of a fishmonger, one of two children in this public grave. Also buried here was Jane Rose 66, a widow, who lived with three grown up sons. The eldest was a metalsmith, the two younger table knife hafters. Three other women were buried in the same plot: Catherine Robert, Mary Bell and Phoebe Jacques. Catherine Roberts, 60, was also a widow. Mary Bell was only 37. She had begun her working life at 14, as the only servant of a coffee house keeper and his large family in Birmingham, but ten years later she was married to Francis Bell, a railway porter and had a son. By 1881 the family had increased to four children between the ages of 12 and 3, and Francis was now recorded as Frank and his occupation was "horse keeper". Mary Bell died three years later. Phoebe Jacques also went out to work while a teenager as the sole servant at the home of a commercial clerk catering for four adults and three children under three. Ten years later she was living at home with her mother and brother, who was a silver piercer. It is not known what happened to her brother but in 1891 her mother, still alive at 80, was "living on parish pay."

Sarah Cheshire was buried in the Anglican area, Section X2, Plot 40, a public grave.

Minnie Clarke

Early September 1917 saw a grisly find under the cellar flagstones of a house in Ashdell Road. This was the small body of Kenneth Clarke, aged 5 months, badly decomposed with its fingers eaten away by rats. The police began to look for Minnie aged 22 years, a servant at the house, who had given birth in January, but whose baby had not been seen since June. She had disappeared and was naturally suspected of killing her child. A description was circulated, including the information that Minnie was "fond of the company of soldiers and may frequent the vicinity of barracks."

Minnie was soon found at 207 Chippinghouse Road and arrested on a charge of wilful murder.

More of this "sensational Sheffield crime" story unfolded at the Coroner's Court a few days later and was reported in the *Sheffield Daily Independent* 8th September 1917. It appeared that Minnie had registered the father of the baby as a soldier, and believed herself to be married, though the marriage turned out to be bigamous. She gave her child to her mother to care for but had removed him from her mother's care when he  was five months old, claiming that she had found someone to adopt the child. Minnie and her mother argued in court about the exact circumstances, with Minnie's accusation that her mother had "sent me a threatening letter that if I didn't take it, you would leave it". The coroner commented, "I think the jury and I will understand that neither the grandmother nor mother wanted this baby very badly".

Minnie denied murdering Kenneth, claiming that he had died while in bed beside her and that she had awoken to find him stiff and cold. She claimed that it was fear that made her bury the baby in the cellar. Whether Minnie's assertion was true or not remains a mystery. The body was too badly composed for the doctor to establish the cause of death, and an open verdict was returned.

Kenneth Clarke was buried in the Nonconformist area, Section T, Plot 77, a public grave behind the Nonconformist chapel, now known as the Samuel Worth Chapel.

Elizabeth Firth

The 1871 Census records that Elizabeth Firth, aged 40, was living on Brick Lane with her husband George, a table knife hafter, and six children, ranging in age from 14 to 8 months. No occupation was recorded for Elizabeth. Three years later George died and was buried in R 57, a public grave. With young children to feed, Elizabeth found work as a cleaner. According to the *Sheffield and Rotherham Independent* 30 August 1875, among those she worked for was William Smedley, a 54-year-old table knife hafter. He had lost his wife the previous year and was now rapidly losing his sight as well. Soon Elizabeth was staying over at William's house two or three nights a week, leaving early in the morning, and the arrangement continued for about eight months, despite the disapproval of William's grown-up children. But then they quarrelled. William told Elizabeth's son that he wanted to marry her. He told Elizabeth that her older children were well able to look after the younger ones, but Elizabeth apparently refused to leave them.

For two months William lived alone at his house in Apple Street until he decided he would have to give it up and go to his married daughter. The following night, having spent part of the day with his grandchildren, he left his daughter's house, and met Elizabeth on her way home from her work. They agreed to go for a drink together. Perhaps William hoped to persuade her to change her mind. Elizabeth told her son she would be about three quarters of an hour. She and William went first to the Bay Horse, Westbar Green, where they stayed talking companionably and drinking a pint of beer each. At around ten o'clock they left and went to the Harrow Inn where they were served with a glass of gin and a glass of whiskey, before leaving half an hour later. Witnesses agreed that the couple seemed sober and calm. Not long afterwards, at around 11.00pm, Sarah Nutton, the wife of an edge tool striker, saw them standing and talking beneath a streetlamp in Apple Street, where William Smedley had his house. She could not hear what he said, but she heard Elizabeth say "No" and "No, never". They had not seemed to be quarrelling. At this point Sarah Nutton heard a noise, as if something had hit her shutter, so she opened her door. William Smedley was running away, and at that moment, Elizabeth, still standing under the streetlamp, fell forward onto her face, blood pooling around her head.

An hour later William Smedley gave himself up to the police. He confessed to killing her "to my sorrow" with a razor, and then ate the bread he had bought earlier. His right hand was covered in blood. He had cut her throat; the blow was so fierce and the blood loss so great that she died within two minutes. When William Smedley's daughter asked him why he had done it, he said because he loved her and later, in prison, that he had been jealous and not in his right mind.

The funeral took place a few days later. The body was removed from the Greaves Hotel, where it had originally been taken, to her house in Bailey Street. A large silent crowd had collected, filling the street, but it dispersed as the relatives followed the hearse in procession to the cemetery, where the service was read by the Rev J. Flather.

William Smedley was sent for trial, found guilty of the murder of Elizabeth Firth 3rd December, and hanged on 21st December 1875. The newspapers reported that he died penitent.

It is not known what happened to Elizabeth's older children, or her youngest, but Mark, the second youngest, was in Sheffield Union Workhouse, Pitsmoor, in 1881. By 1891 he was living with Phineas, two years older, and his family, in Ecclesfield. The brothers were coal miners. Mark remained a coal miner, and by 1911 was married with three children, two having died young.

Elizabeth Firth is buried in the Nonconformist area, Section E, Plot 161, a public grave.

Sarah Grace

The inquest into Sarah's death tells a sorry tale. She lived a life of poverty, and died on Thursday 10th November 1846 of internal haemorrhaging, although the inquest and post-mortem, reported in the *Sheffield Independent* 14 November 1846, did not reveal the circumstances of the haemorrhage. Her death, it was thought, had been accelerated "by want of food." Sarah was a "woman of dissolute habits", whose occupation was binding boots and shoes. Her house was filthy and "almost entirely destitute of any furniture". She slept on a mattress and straw and had no bedclothes. On 9 November she became ill and her friend Ann- described at the inquest as "a girl of bad character"- took her to the workhouse in a cab. She died the next day. The burial record does not record her age.

Sarah Grace was buried in the Nonconformist area, Section N, Plot 48, a public grave at the side of the Nonconformist Chapel, now known as the Samuel Worth Chapel.

Evangeline Lothian Guest

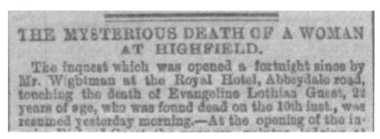

THE MYSTERIOUS DEATH OF A WOMAN AT HIGHFIELD.

The inquest which was opened a fortnight since by Mr. Wightman at the Royal Hotel, Abbeydale road, touching the death of Evangeline Lothian Guest, 22 years of age, who was found dead on the 10th inst., was resumed yesterday morning.—At the opening of the in-

Evangeline Lothian Guest, nee Farrar, died in 1879 aged 22. The only traces left of her life are a marriage record, for 1877, a burial record, and newspaper reports of the tragedy and the inquest into her death (*Sheffield Telegraph* 14 and 28 October 1879). According to her husband Richard, they had gone to bed in the room they rented on London Road at 11.00. The baby woke at 11.30 and as his wife was "asleep and snoring" he soothed the child himself. When the baby next woke, at 8.00, and his wife did not respond immediately, he looked closer, and realised that she was dead. She had previously been in good health but not very strong; she had fainting fits. Mr Abraham Jones, a neighbouring chemist and their former landlord, came and administered brandy, ammonia to the nose and hot water to wrists and hands, but when the doctor, Mr James, arrived, he pronounced life extinct. Even after the post-mortem he was not able to give a precise cause of death. There was congestion of the brain, lungs and liver which might have been consistent with some form of poisoning, and there were traces of opium, but nothing sufficient to cause death. In his opinion she was in good health, not delicate, although "slight", and badly nourished. There was no fat at all in the body.

Others were questioned. Their current landlord, Joseph Jones, a joiner, thought that Evangeline had "seen trouble and some knocking about" but his wife thought Evangeline 'very lively'. She had never heard her complain or quarrel with her husband. Their former landlady, the wife of the chemist, had a different story. She and Evangeline had been friendly, and Evangeline was used to dropping in after they had moved, when the chemist's wife often gave her something to eat. Evangeline had said she wanted to leave the marriage, because her husband stayed out drinking a great deal and brought very little money home, so there wasn't enough food. Apparently, she had also said that she would rather harm herself than stay with her husband. Questioned, the chemist's wife admitted that she could easily have found and taken away some opium, which was kept with other medication on open shelves.

Mr Wightman, the coroner, ordered a chemical analysis of the organs. This was carried out by Alfred Allan, who explained that opium very quickly disappeared in the body, but he had found traces of a weak solution on the dead woman's sleeve, and traces also in some of the organs. What had been detected was not enough to cause death, but it was possible that there had been more than was found. Opium had certainly been taken before death. He had found no evidence of any other poisons.

The jury's verdict carried a damning comment: "Found dead in bed on the 10th inst., having recently taken opium, but how or why taken or administered there is no evidence to show, and the said jury further say that Richard Guest the husband is highly censured for his neglect and ill treatment."

Very little more is known about Evangeline's husband Richard, but Richard's parents, Richard Snr. and Mary Ann Guest, gave her a place in the family plot, memorialised her on the headstone, and made a home for the baby, Henry Richard Christian Guest, who followed his grandfather and great grandfather's trade of painting and decorating. The 1911 Census shows that he returned to Devonshire St where his family had lived for three generations. He and his wife Annie had two children, a son born in 1901 called Ernest Richard, and a daughter born in 1905 - Eva Annie, named for both his mother and his wife.

Evangline Lothian Guest is buried with Richard Guest's parents and some of his siblings in the Anglican area, Section J, Plot 14 below the Anglican chapel. The Anglican area was cleared of monuments and headstones when Sheffield City Council took over the site in 1978.

Ada Meeson

Ada's death was something of a local "cause celebre" which drew lurid headlines like "The Sheffield Murder" and "Sequel to Illicit Love Affair" from the *Sheffield Independent* of March 1905.

Ada, about 28 years old, of slight build, had been a lodger at the home of Mr and Mrs Battle on Clarence Street. She had lived apart from her husband Tom since he left to fight in South Africa several years before. When he returned, he found that she was in a relationship with a man called Edward Dalton. Edward Dalton frequently visited Ada at Clarence Street.

About 11pm on the fateful evening, the Battles came home after an evening out to discover their lodger's body in the kitchen "all of a heap upon the floor" with a terrible wound to the throat and neck. The place was "a shambles" and covered with blood.

An unnamed man stated that his brother had confessed to the crime and was consequently "offing it to the dams". Despite an extensive police search no one could be found and Dalton's whereabouts were a mystery too. However, a man giving his name as Coldwell was later charged with being drunk and disorderly, though he was identified as Dalton by people who knew him as the man seen in the company of Ada. Coldwell/Dalton was suspected of causing Ada's death, and attempted suicide by cutting his throat, thereby initiating a special investigation by the Watch Committee, a local government body which oversaw policing. The inquest into Ada's death was adjourned until Dalton was fit to attend.

Subsequently Edwin James Dalton, a stoker aged 44, was charged with Ada's murder. *The Advertiser*, 10 May 1905, also reported that he was found guilty "under strong provocation". The sentence was later commuted to penal servitude for life. Ada's

THE CLARENCE STREET TRAGEDY.

Funeral of the Victim.

At the Sheffield General Cemetery, yesterday, the remains of Mrs. Ada Meeson, the unfortunate victim of the Clarence street murder, were laid to rest. A number of police were in attendance, a large crowd being anticipated. Up to yesterday morning the body had been lying in the City Mortuary, where ... was removed immediately after the murder, and

funeral took place from her husband's house on 16 March 1905. From newspaper reports this was an occasion to be relished as the anticipation of a large crowd necessitated the attendance of several police. Although the crowd wasn't as great as anticipated, only about 500 people, principally from surrounding streets, by the time the cortege reached the cemetery numbers had doubled to nearly a thousand. They were to be disappointed as only family mourners and representative of the press were admitted.

Ada Meeson was buried in the Nonconformist area, Section T, Plot 367, a public grave behind the Samuel Worth Chapel.

Elizabeth Neild (Nield)

Elizabeth Neild, wife of James Neild, machine maker and furniture broker, was tragically discovered suspended by the neck on 7th June 1847.

The *Sheffield Independent's* report of the inquest on 12 June, revealed that she had "been for ten or twelve years past an habitual drunkard" and "within the last few months she had seldom been sober for more than a day together". She had parted from her husband several times because of her "disgusting habit", and during the week before her death there had been a quarrel which resulted in her husband threatening to turn her out. Despite a promise made in front of a neighbour that she would abstain from "intoxicating liquors" if her husband forgave her, the following day and every day until her death, Elizabeth was said to be" in a beastly state of intoxication".

The jury returned a verdict that "the deceased had committed suicide in a fit of temporary insanity brought on by excessive drinking". The judgemental tone of this sad story perhaps illustrates how suicide could only be integrated within the Victorian conventions of death by emphasising character flaws which result in temporary mental imbalance. It is also interesting to note that the newspaper item following this one is also of suicide as a consequence of drunkenness, this time by a 60-year-old man which allowed that "these drunken fits" were followed by "illness and depression of the spirits." The tone of the second report is

27

more factual and less denigrating than in the coverage of Elizabeth Nield. Drunkenness in women seems to have aroused much stronger public condemnation.

Elizabeth Neild was buried in the Nonconformist area, Section B, Plot 46, a public grave.

Ann Parkin

Ann is described in the burial records as a "pauper", an unfortunate condition all too common in single women who, when elderly, were unable to provide for themselves. Although we don't know anything else about Ann's circumstances, there was great interest surrounding her burial. Our source is the *Sheffield Independent* of 4 May 1881 and the headline of the article reads "Extraordinary interment at the Sheffield cemetery". It appears that Ann was deaf.

The article goes on to say that she was a spinster aged 32 years, although burial records tell us that she was in fact aged 72, and that she had died in the new Workhouse at Pitsmoor on 29th April 1881. She did not have any family, but her "similarly afflicted" friends provided a more decent coffin than the usual one which would have been provided for a pauper's funeral. There were twelve mourners, and the service was conducted by Mr George Stephenson, Superintendent of the 'Sheffield Association in aid of the Adult Deaf and Dumb', which was established in 1861. He conducted the burial service using "signs". This was the first burial wholly conducted using sign language, though the article reports that Mr Stephenson had previously interpreted at funerals where "deaf mutes" had been present. Mr Stephenson died in April 1924 and was buried in the Anglican area of the Cemetery. Ann was buried in a Public Grave in the Nonconformist area of the Cemetery. This grave contains 29 other burials.

Ann Parkin is buried in the Nonconformist area, Section T, Plot 143, a public grave.

Women and Childbirth

Margaret Green

Margaret Green, who died in 1869, is another of the many women in the Cemetery whose lives are barely visible to twenty first century visitors. The stone from her grave, moved to the lower level of the catacombs after the Anglican area was cleared in 1979/80, memorialises the deaths of ten of her children who died in infancy.

Margaret married in 1842, when she was 16. Neither Margaret nor her husband, Thomas, could write their own names. In the 1840s and 50s Thomas worked as a saw grinder, and in the 1850s and 60s as a pork butcher. Their lives as parents were particularly tragic. The first child, John, was born in 1842 and died aged three and a half, of croup. Harriet, born in 1848, died of bronchitis, aged 7 months, and George, born in 1844, died aged five of "inflammation of the brain". Thomas, born in 1850, died of convulsions aged 13 months, Sarah Ann died nine months later, aged only six weeks, also of convulsions. Mary Ann, born in 1846, died in 1854 of scarlatina, aged seven, Ada of bronchitis in 1863 aged 9 months, Albert of pneumonia in 1866 aged 23 months, Rosetta of diarrhoea and convulsions in 1866 aged five months, and Augustus, their last child together, born when Margaret was 42, died of "debility from birth" in 1867 aged six days. The cycle of birth, suffering and death must have seemed never ending.

Margaret herself died during an operation for breast cancer. Chloroform was available in 1869, the year of her death, but it is not known if it was available to her. The inscription on the stone perhaps implies that it was not: "She was brought as a lamb to the slaughter, as a sheep before her shearers is dumb, so she openeth not her mouth."

Three daughters and one son survived to adulthood. Adelaide, born in 1853, died of meningitis aged 35, leaving a husband and daughter. Emily, born in 1856, was a milliner's apprentice in 1871. Ernest, born in the same year that another child died, grew up and was still living with his father in 1881, when he was recorded as being a labourer. The last child to survive Margaret was Florence, born in 1861, who was seven when her mother died.

Thomas remarried and the first child of his second marriage was born two years later. He lived to be 81.

Despite all the names memorialised on the headstone, there are only three bodies in the grave purchased by Thomas, in January 1870, when he was a pork butcher at 108 West Bar: Margaret herself, Thomas, who died in 1903, and Maud Beatrice Green who died aged 4 years and 6 months in 1883. She was one of the four children of Thomas' second marriage, and at the time of her death Thomas gave his occupation as cattle dealer. At the time of his own death his occupation was given as "master grinder (retired)".

Margaret's story is a testament to the lives of all the women who struggled with the difficulties of inner city living, poor sanitation and constant childbirth during the first half of the nineteenth century.

Her story is not unusual. The mortality rate for young children in nineteenth century cities was depressingly high. There are many other memorial inscriptions in the Cemetery listing multiple deaths of children within individual families; the many children in the common graves have no memorial. One public grave, B 89 in the Nonconformist area, used in 1841, contains 41 people, 37 of whom are children, and 36 of those are under five years old.

Of the eight children of Louise **Lindley** and her husband Henry, a cashier, six died young between 1844 and 1876 - of whooping cough (Lucy Ann, 12 weeks), premature birth (twins Emily and Alice, 2 hours), lung inflammation (Frederick, one year) and "decline" (Lucy, 4 weeks.) Causes of death for Louisa Ann, 18 months, Herbert, aged 6, and Florence 13, are not given in our records. One son, Thomas, outlived both his parents, and one daughter. *They were buried in the Nonconformist area, Section FF, Plot 14.*

Ann and Benjamin **Howgate**, a mark maker and agent for Derby Ale, lived at Brightside. They lost eight children between 1847 and 1869, the oldest at 6, the others at two years or younger. Sarah Hannah died aged 19 months of lung inflammation, Ann aged 3 of "inflammation" and four children of diarrhoea and dysentery. Three daughters and a son survived into adulthood. *The family were buried in the Nonconformist area, Section L, Plot 124.*

Martha and Robert **Clarborough**, a bricklayer, lost six children between the ages of 20 days and 11 years between 1837 and 1855.

Four other children may have outlived their parents. *They were buried in the Nonconformist area Section G, Plot 42.*

Being part of the middle class was no protection: Sarah and John Yoeman **Cowlishaw,** a successful businessman, lost five children who died between the ages of 5 and 13 between 1861 and 1877: causes of death included bronchitis, pneumonia, diphtheria and meningitis. Three sons and one daughter survived them. *The Cowlishaws were buried in the Anglican area Section M, Plot 130/131.*

Margaret Green was buried in the cleared Anglican area, Section Q1, Plot 178. The headstone now lies flat on the lower tier of the catacombs.

Women in Business

Mary Andrews

Mary Jane Andrews, born in 1845 in Whittlesea, Cambridgeshire, was one of six known children of William, a joiner, and Bethia Andrews. Unlike her three sisters, Mary did not marry and was listed as a bonnet maker in the 1861 and 1871 Census but as a dressmaker in 1881. Until then she was living with her parents, who in 1881 were catering for three lodgers to make ends meet. Mary's father died in 1883 and her mother in 1888. It is not known where she was in 1891 and 1901, but in 1911 Mary was listed as head of the household at 54 Wolseley Road, and living with her were her niece and nephew, Irene Kidney aged 21, a milliner's assistant, and Herbert, 19, described as a carver in a restaurant.

Mary died 3rd December 1921 and was buried in a plot bought by her sister Sarah's husband, Edward Birks, a butcher, on the death of their infant son in 1862. Another infant son was buried here five years later, and Mary's parents, William and Bethia Andrews. However, the only person memorialised on the headstone is Mary, 'In loving memory of Mary Jane Andrews who fell asleep December 3rd, 1921, aged 71 years.'

Mary Jane Andrews is buried in the Nonconformist area, in Section K Plot 61, with other family members.

Harriet Barber, Mary Ann Barber

I & J Barber, a cutlery firm, was run by Harriet Barber for almost twenty years, and by her daughter in law, Mary Ann Barber, for 16 years. The business had been established by Isaac Barber in the 1820s; his son James, apprenticed as a cutler, later became his business partner. Isaac died in 1854, and his wife Mary was able to purchase a grave in a prominent position in the General Cemetery.

She was later buried there herself, although she is not mentioned on the headstone.

The business passed to James, but he died only five years later, in 1859, when his children were aged 11 and 4, and from that point it was managed by James' wife Harriet. In 1861 she was described as a "cutlery manufacturer "of Broad Lane, employing 16 hands,

and in 1871 19 men and 6 boys. Her son Edward, then 23, was described as her manager. In 1881 the census shows that she was still living in Broad Lane and still a cutlery manufacturer. Edward had married, to Mary Ann, and was also described as a cutlery manufacturer. In White's Trade Directory 1879 both he and his mother are listed as cutlery manufacturers, their firm I & J Barber. It seems likely that by 1881 Edward had taken over much of the responsibility. Harriet left her home in Broad Lane for lodgings in Nursery Street and then went to live with her daughter, where she died in 1887. She left £367 11s in her will.

Edward had already died in 1885 leaving £1,014 2s 8d for his wife and ten-year-old son. Mary Ann took over the business and ran it for 16 years, from 1885 to 1901, before dying suddenly at the age of only 50. She was very much a proactive owner, defending her right to the sole use of the name "Edward Barber" (Sheffield Independent, 4th March, 1893), and moving the business from Broad Lane to the Era Works in Wheeldon Street. I & J Barber still specialised in spring knives and razors but also produced household cutlery which was exported to Ireland. At the time of her death, she had just moved to The Grange, Sandygate, which still exists, a reflection of her success in business.

Mary Ann left assets of £40,110 3s. 10d. I & J Barber was inherited by her son but by 1914 it had been acquired by another company. Neither Harriet nor Mary were buried in the Barber grave, Harriet because she had moved away to live with her daughter, and Mary Ann because she had bought a plot for her husband at Ecclesall and so joined him there.

Harriet Barber's husband, mother-in-law and father-in-law are buried in the Nonconformist area, Section HH, Plot 188

Jemima Binns

NEW FUNERAL CARRIAGE Mrs JEMIMA BINNS respectfully announces, that she has fitted up a convenient FUNERAL CARRIAGE capable of carrying, in addition to the Corpse, 14 Mourners, which she will be enabled to Let out on very reasonable Terms.
In addition to the above, a HEARSE and MOURNING COACHES will be Let out as usual.
Mrs. BINNS tenders her sincere thanks for the valued patronage she has received since the death of her lamented Husband, and trusts that her future efforts to merit the continued favours of her Friends will ensure their generous support.
CABS and PARTY CARRIAGES at a moment's notice. South street, Sheffield moor, Oct. 5, 1849.

Jemima Binns was the mother of eight children, ranging in age from sixteen to one year, when her husband, Joseph, a coach hire proprietor, died in 1841 aged 48, following a driving accident. Joseph had had the foresight to write a will in which he hoped that "my wife shall carry on my business as a coach proprietor." Perhaps Jemima had already helped in the business before he was killed. In any event, she fulfilled his wishes admirably and ran the business until 1865, three years before her own death, despite the deaths of her two eldest children.

Her three sons all worked for her as drivers, but Thomas, the eldest, died aged 21, six years after his father, when he was drowned. He had taken a group out to Chatsworth for the day. He and another cab driver, having left the horses at Baslow, went back into park to cool off in the Derwent. But Thomas could not swim and against the advice of his friend, tried to cross to the other side. The river was deep in the middle. He sank and could not be rescued in time. The *Sheffield Independent*, 21 August 1847, commented that he "had been of great assistance to his mother" since her husband's death.

Jemima continued to run the business until she retired 18 years later in 1865. Everything was sold by public auction, including 24 horses, a range of carriages, a hearse, mourning coaches and two omnibuses. The advertisement in the Sheffield Independent included the note: "The Coaching Business has been successfully carried on by Mrs Binns and her late husband for upwards of thirty years"' The casual reader might not have realized that Jemima Binns had run "one of the most popular Coaching and Cab establishments in the district" entirely without her husband for 24 of those years.

She died in the spring of 1868, leaving less than £800. Her two eldest children predeceased her, and of her three sons only James, the youngest, outlived her. He worked as a bus driver (horse drawn) for the rest of his life, married to Hannah, one of the children of Alder man Thomas Burch (formerly Mycock), whose tall monument stands at the top of the chapel steps.

Inscribed on her monument are the words: "She looketh well to the ways of her household and eateth not the bread of idleness."

Jemima Binns is buried in the Nonconformist area, Section H, Plot 169.

Annie Elizabeth Burr

Annie Elizabeth Butler was born in 1857, the eldest daughter of Charles and Elizabeth Butler, nee Smith. In 1861 the family were living at 81 Cemetery Road with one servant. Charles was a master confectioner. By 1871 the family were at 79 Fargate with three daughters, aged 12, 11 and 2. Charles' business flourished; by the beginning of the 1880s he could afford two servants, and employed four men as well as his wife and daughters.

Unfortunately, Annie fell in love with one of those men, Henry Burton, believed to be a widower, and in 1880 they ran away together and married. Charles did not give up on his daughter. Enquiries were made; it was discovered that far from being a widower, Henry Burton had a wife and two children, all very much alive. Henry was committed for trial at Leeds Assizes, and subsequently sentenced to eighteen months' imprisonment with hard labour. The case became a sensation: newspapers all over the country reported the story in detail.

Annie returned to the family home and to work in her father's business. Less than three years later she married a Manchester confectioner, Frederick Burr, who acted as agent for his father-in-law. Frederick died in 1888 aged only 29. Annie remained in Manchester, running the business, "Butler and Burr", and in 1901 was still listed as a confectioner, living with a housekeeper and two shop assistants. Frederick and Annie had no children. Charles Butler died in 1898 and by 1911 Annie had returned to Sheffield and taken control. She did not remarry, and died in 1913, aged 55. A notice in the Sheffield Daily Telegraph referred to her taking over her father's business and described her as "a lady who, in an unobtrusive way, assisted many who were in need of help, and was also a subscriber to various public charities."

Annie Elizabeth Burr is buried with her husband and other family members in the Anglican area, Section S, Plot 171. The monument is near the path which leads from the Anglican Chapel to Montague Street.

Hannah and Mary Cadman

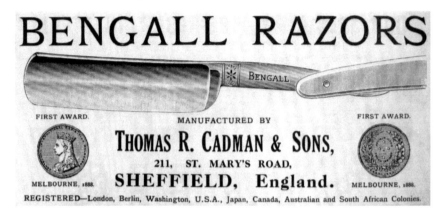

The trademark BENGALL was first granted to Luke Cadman in 1748 and stayed with the family until the closure of the business in 1965. Luke's sons, Luke Jun. and Peter, joined the family business. The BENGALL mark established an international reputation in the late eighteenth and early nineteenth century, with business locations including Fargate, Surrey Street and Carver Street. Peter married Hannah Staniland in 1793. Widows of Freemen of Cutlers were able to carry on the family business using their husband's corporate mark and after Peter's death Hannah was listed in the 1820's as "manufacturer" of Bengall razors from Cadman's Yard, Fargate. In 1821 she attempted to defend the family's trade mark when another manufacturer began using the word 'BENGOL'. Hannah "razor manufacturer" died in 1828 aged 55 and was buried in St Peter's churchyard.

The business then passed to Hannah and Peter's second son Alfred, but he died in 1841 from "brain fever" aged 39, and his wife, Mary continued to run the business. In the 1851 census she was listed as a razor manufacturer, employing eight men. She ran the business until the 1860s, when her sons Peter, Thomas and Alfred took over.

The monumental inscription reads:

> In memory of Alfred Cadman, who died October 5, 1841, aged 39 years,
>
> Also Hannah Cadman sister of the above who died April 23 1850 aged 54 years.
>
> Also Peter Cadman, eldest son of Alfred Cadman died July 31 1860, aged 31 years.
>
> Also Mary, relict of Alfred Cadman who died August 23 1877 aged 74 years

Mary Cadman is buried in the Nonconformist area, Section B, Plot 123.

Mary Fawcett, Marianne and Martha Fawcett

Marianne and Martha Fawcett were the daughters of Mary and John Fawcett, who married in 1795 and had six children. After John died, Mary married George Wightman and had at least one more child, Benjamin Wightman, who became a successful Sheffield solicitor.

Widowed for a second time, Mary Fawcett Wightman with her two Fawcett daughters acquired Belfield House and established a boarding and day academy for "young ladies". There was an advertisement for the school in the *Sheffield Independent* 21st January 1826 in the name of the "Misses Fawcett". They were still there at the time of the 1841 Census when there were 25 pupils between the ages of 10 and 15. Marianne and Martha were then aged 39 and 30. Perhaps Marianne's health was beginning to fail because by 1844 they had left, and the academy was then run by their successors, the Misses Barlow. (*Sheffield Independent* 29th June 1844) Marianne died in 1848 aged 46, which was when Mary purchased the grave plot.

By 1851 Mary had moved from Belfield House to Broom Hall Park with Martha and one servant and both Mary and Martha were described as retired schoolmistresses. Staying with them 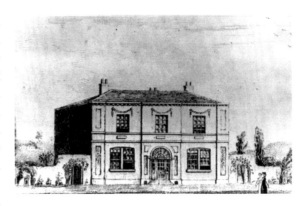 was four-year-old Mary Alice Wightman, Mary's granddaughter, the daughter of Benjamin. Mary died in 1860, described in the death notice as the widow of George Wightman and the mother of Alderman (William)Fawcett, who died himself in 1864 and who is also buried in the Cemetery. Martha moved to Scarborough. In 1861 she was boarding with Thomas Plowman and family, still described as a retired governess, where she died in 1865. Like her sister, she was unmarried. Her will – she left "under £300" - was proved by her half-brother Benjamin Wightman, the sole executor, by then retired.

Mary Fawcett and her daughters are buried in the Nonconformist area of the cemetery, in Section J, Plot J 5.

Mary Snape

Mary was born in Ecclesfield in 1819. Her husband, Edward, was a table knife manufacturer. By 1841 they were living in Charles Street and had a workshop there with another cutler called William Robinson who may have been Mary's brother. Edward died in 1850 aged 34; the grave in which he was buried had been bought by him in 1845 when their daughter Maria died aged 4. Two years after Edward's death their son William also died, aged 7. Mary, left with two daughters to provide for, continued in the cutlery trade. In 1861 she was living in Brittain Street and was listed as a spring knife manufacturer, living next door to William Robinson who worked in the same business and employed two men and three boys. Mary described herself as a "cutler" and was listed as such in the directory for the next two decades. She retired in 1891 and was recorded as living with her daughter, Emily, who was a blade and fork flyer. Mary died aged 78 in January 1897.

Mary Snape is buried with her husband Edward, and two of their children, in the Nonconformist area, Section L, Plot 155.

Charlotte Taylor

Charlotte Taylor ran an anvil making business. Born in Sheffield in 1827, she was the daughter of Harriet and Matthias Davenport, a cutler, before marrying anvil maker William Taylor in 1850. The couple had eight children. In 1879 William died and left the sole charge of the anvil making business to his wife Charlotte, when she was 52. Two years later the 1881 census taker mistakenly put Charlotte down as "Charles" Taylor anvil maker, perhaps because they assumed the head of the business would be a man. Charlotte ran the business successfully for more than twenty years, employing other anvil makers, including at least one son. Her daughter Jane was her bookkeeper. Charlotte died, still in charge, at the age of 77.

Charlotte Taylor is buried with her husband and three adult children in the cleared Anglican area of the cemetery, in SectionV1, Plot 94. The headstone has been moved to the lower tier of the catacombs. .

Self-Supporting Women

Olivia Bennett

Olivia Bennet died in 1905 and is one of the few single women of this period to be given a published obituary. The *Sheffield Telegraph,* 18 February 1905, described her in glowing terms:

> There passed away yesterday morning, at 7 Eyre Street, Miss Olivia Bennett, in her 87th year a dear old lady who may be truly said to have record of a blameless life.
>
> Seventy years ago, she, with the late Dr Sutton, Vicar of Sheffield, opened a Sunday School, the first in connection with the Parish Church.
>
> The school in School Croft, was hired for the purpose, and this lady continued her good work for 62 years.
>
> She was born in York Street, removing to Eyre Street 53 years ago, where she lived until yesterday. This is a good certificate for the healthiness of Sheffield.
>
> Her friends were many, and to those who appreciate refinement and a high standard of religious life, combined with a happy and cheerful disposition, her friendship was considered privilege.
>
> Her mother and father were natives of Wentworth, her grandfather holding an important position in connection with Earl Fitzwilliam's collieries.

Olivia was born in York Street, Sheffield. She lived for at least 50 years at 7, Eyre Street, with her older sister Mary, also unmarried. They were both described as dressmakers on census returns but they sometimes took in a single lady boarder. They always maintained one servant to help in the house. Mary died in 1878, but Olivia stayed on in their home, still taking in boarders when she was 83.

Olivia's work in starting a Sunday School in 1835 and continuing to teach there for 62 years was a significant achievement and would have been of great value to her community. Until the 1870 Education Act, Sunday Schools  of all denominations were one of the more accessible routes to a basic education for poorer children. Several well-known, self-made Sheffield men were grateful to their Sunday school for that early education.

Olivia Bennett is buried with her sister Mary in the cleared Anglican area, Section B3, Plot 100.

Elizabeth Gill

Elizabeth, born in Sheffield in 1820, was part of the overlooked and large cohort of women in Sheffield who worked as 'buffer girls'. Buffer girls buffed or polished cutlery and other metal goods to create a smooth, polished surface. It was hard, dirty work and to protect themselves and their clothing, the women wore overalls, head scarves, neck scarves and brown paper aprons. Elizabeth Gill, married to Edwin Gill, an edge tool grinder, was described as a silver burnisher in 1851, 1861, 1871 and 1881. They had nine children: two died in infancy but all their other daughters became buffers and their sons became grinders. Both were necessary jobs in the metal work industries and provided work for a great many people. Neither were well paid, and a large family meant that everyone who could, had to work. Elizabeth must have managed the finances well; unusually for a woman in her situation she was able to leave £94 and seven pence to her heirs. She died in March 1890 at the age of 70.

Elizabeth Gill is buried with her husband and three of their children in the Anglican area, Section O1, Plot 157. The headstone has been moved to the lower tier of the catacombs.

Emma May

Emma May died aged 48 in 1895 and was buried in a public grave in the Anglican section. As with all public graves, there would have been no stone to mark the spot. Emma May was a widow, and her address was given as 192 Hanover Street.

192 Hanover Street was also the address of William Watson, an anvil maker and his two children, Elsie, 11, and Charles 7. Emma May was described as the housekeeper in the 1891 census. Also in the house were William May, 23, a printer compositor, and Frederick May, 21, a wine merchant's porter. They were both described as "lodgers". All the Mays were born in Torquay, Devon.

Emma, maiden name Barnes, had married William Piper May, an Ordinary Seaman in the Royal Navy, in 1864 in Newton Abbot, when he was 23 and Emma was 17. Their eldest son William was born four years later, and their second son Frederick in 1870, but William Snr was lost at sea on 7 September 1870 when the ship on which he was serving, the HMS Captain, capsized in a heavy squall, and went down in three minutes.

The ship, of a new design, was on her fourth trial voyage, travelling in company with ten other ships. According to the Hastings and St Leonards Observer 17 September 1870, not a single officer survived the disaster. At least 473 men died. Captain Cole, the designer, also died. At the official inquiry, some of the 18 surviving crew members suggested that 'iron masts and the heavy armoured turret, with its six 25 tonne guns, rendered the ship top heavy.' The official verdict found that "the ship had been capsized by the pressure of sail, assisted by the heave of the sea, but that such sail would not have been sufficient to endanger a vessel endowed with the proper amount of stability". Also "there had been great departure from the

original designs, whereby the draught water had been increased two feet, and her freeboard diminished to a corresponding extent". (*Hampshire Telegraph* 10 September 1904). It was a Portsmouth ship and in one street alone thirty wives were widowed by the disaster. The loss of the HMS Captain attracted nationwide sympathy and a fund set up for the relief of the families of those drowned.

The tragedy left Emma alone at 23, with a small naval pension, and two tiny children to support. The 1871 Census showed her still in Torquay, her occupation listed as 'milliner'. Ten years later both William, 13, and Frederick, 11, were boarders at the Royal Patriotic Asylum for Boys, Wandsworth Common. The Royal Patriotic Fund was inaugurated by Queen Victoria in 1854 during the Crimean War to collect donations on behalf of widows and orphans of soldiers, sailors and marines that had died during or as a result of the hostilities. Part of the money raised was used to establish the Royal Victoria Patriotic Asylum for Boys and a sister establishment for girls. However, in 1881 it was decided to close the Asylum for Boys on financial grounds. The children in the school were found places in other institutions or sent to carers with an allowance. It is not known what happened next to William and Frederick, or how and why the family came to Sheffield. Was Emma impelled to move far away from all sea faring associations? Or did she and her younger son accompany William, who had found an employment opportunity? Emma never remarried and, it would seem, devoted her relatively short life to her sons' welfare. In 1901, William, still a printer and compositor, was married and had a two-year-old son, William, and a William May died in Sheffield in 1941. It is not known what happened to Frederick, but a Frederick May died in Plymouth in 1958.

Emma May is buried in the Anglican area, in Section W2, Plot 55, a public grave.

Louisa Oates

Although we do not know anything about Louisa's family background, census returns indicate that her life, full of hardships, represented that of a Victorian working-class single woman. In Louisa's case it also meant never having a settled home.

The censuses from 1851 and 1861 show her living at 11 Gell Street, first as a general servant and then as a housekeeper. By 1871 she had moved to East Bank House, Sheffield Park, again as a servant, now aged 56 years. In 1881 she was working as a housekeeper, this time at 40 Washington Road, and finally in 1891 she was listed as a boarder at 41 Mount Pleasant Road, aged 77 years, "living on own means". At least she was spared the workhouse.

Louisa died on 28th November, 1895, aged 82 years and her address is shown as 75 Aberdeen Street. Hers is the only burial in this grave, and the inscription reads: "In loving memory of Louisa Oates who died November 28th, 1895, aged 82 years."

The plot was purchased by Thomas Oates, a "gentleman" of Snape Hill, Dronfield. We have been unable to identify this particular Thomas. There are many "Oates" listed in the burial records.

Louisa Oates is buried in the cleared Anglican area, Section O1, Plot 189.

Frances Mary Rudd

Frances Mary was one of the nine children of Thomas Rudd, a scissor manufacturer, and his wife Frances, and in 1871 the two eldest boys were already working as scissor smiths. Ten years later, much had changed. Frances' father had died and only five children were living at home. Frances Rudd was earning money as a grocer and provision dealer. The two eldest girls were not listed as having paid work, although presumably they provided their mother with support. Frances Mary, then 16, was still described as a scholar. By 1891 she had qualified as a National School teacher and Albert Rudd, her younger brother was a "scissor manager" but they were both boarding with their older sister and brother-in-law, their mother having died. By 1901, at the age of 36, Frances Mary had her own home; a niece, aged 25, was living with her. Frances' occupation was given as "cookery teacher". Frances Mary remained unmarried; had she married she would have been expected to resign from teaching.

During the First World War, 1914 – 1918, her occupation as a cookery teacher would have had particular importance. Before 1914 Britain had become increasingly dependent on imported food but during wartime merchant ships were targeted, and severe weather in 1916 led to a poor harvest, adding to food shortages. Women who could devise nutritious meals from limited ingredients and teach what they knew would have been part of an invaluable female "army", many already serving in many previously traditional male occupations.

Frances Mary Rudd is buried in the cleared Anglican area, Section U, Plot 65.

Mary Scattergood

Most women in the nineteenth century married. It was expected of them; they moved from the family into service, and then moved into even greater service by marrying, having a new baby every second year, their work generally unpaid, although some working-class women were able to supplement the family income by part time work.

Other women chose not to marry. Mary Scattergood seems to have been one of these. She was baptised in Chesterfield, 2nd October

1796, the daughter of Thomas and Alice Scattergood, but very little is known of her life until 1851, when the census return shows that at 54 she was the eldest of three house servants at the Attercliffe home of John Milner, an unmarried man who was a barrister, but at 69 no longer in practice. She was still there in 1861, along with one of the other two house servants. John Milner was then 79, but he presumably died in the following years as the 1871 census shows Mary at Attercliffe Hall, now listed as housekeeper (but also an annuitant) to a "gentlewoman" Elizabeth T. Milner, 63, also unmarried, and Sarah Esther Milner, Elizabeth's sister, aged 53 and unmarried. Mary was then 74, but there were other servants: a groom, a cook, a housemaid and a kitchen maid. Perhaps Elizabeth inherited the Hall and with it Mary, the faithful servant.

By 1881 this group of women had moved to Crescent Road. Elizabeth Milner's sister was no longer with them, but Teresa Roebuck, the cook in 1871, was still employed. There was also a new housemaid but no groom or kitchen maid, and Mary Scattergood was now described as a "boarder" and annuitant. Mary died in July of the same year. Despite being in domestic service all her adult life, she was able to leave £1,861 8s. 6d. in her will, the sole executor being Frank Wever, Savings Bank Actuary. He is listed as the owner of her grave but probably this was paid for out of her estate. She is the only person buried in the plot. Elizabeth died five years later.

The inscription reads: "In memory of Mary Scattergood for many years the faithful housekeeper of the late John Milner Esq of the Hall, Attercliffe, who died July 28th, 1881, aged 85 years."

Mary made a bequest of £18 19s. to the Girls' Charity School in Sheffield.

Mary Scattergood is buried in the cleared Anglican area, Section K1, Plot 53.

Mary Ann Wilkin

The 1851 Census tells us that Mary, born in Edensor, Derbyshire, was a silver burnisher and married to George, a manufacturer's clerk. They were living at 75 Wellington Road. By 1871 Mary, aged 57, had moved to 57 Monmouth Street and was listed as "Head", so we presume she was then a widow. Mary was described as letting "apartments"; her daughter, Rose Hannah, was living with her. There were two boarders: one a tailor's manager from  Lincolnshire, with the intriguing name of Stanton Hunks, and the other Felix Gross, listed as a foreign correspondent from Zurich, Switzerland. Felix would later marry Mary's daughter, Rose.

Two years before Mary's death in 1893, Felix Goss and his wife Rose were living at 4 Collegiate Crescent with their two sons and one servant. Mary was listed as "living on own means" and her place of residence Stoney Middleton, Derbyshire.

Mary died on 27 April 1893 aged 68 years. She was buried in the cleared Anglican area of the Cemetery with her daughter Rose who died aged 48, the following year.

Mary is buried in the Anglican area, Section U1, plot 5, with her daughter. The stone has been moved to the right hand side of the main drive. The plot was owned by Felix Gross.

Women in the Arts

Jane Elizabeth Callender

Jane Elizabeth Callender first married James Livesey, who in 1871 was a commercial clerk in Birmingham. They had two children then, Florence, aged three, and James, six months but ten years later Jane was the actress wife of Edwin Romaine Callender, a tragedian and theatre manager. Her daughter Florence Livesey was living with them, and they had three more children of their own – Dora, 7, Edwin, 5, and Edwina, 11 months. Florence  Livesey's brother James, 10, and his brother Walter, a year younger, were living with their Livesey grandparents.

Jane clearly embraced the life of the theatre, where women were less restricted by conventions, since she must have begun working as an actor soon after she met Edwin. They do not seem to have toured as much as some other theatrical families, but Dora was born in Dawlish and Edwin in Newcastle. Their two youngest, Edwina and Alfred, were born in Sheffield, while Edwin was lessee and manager of the Theatre Royal, Tudor Street, from 1880 to 1884. Throughout this period the couple acted on stage despite the death of Edwina at two and a half. Edwina was the first of the family to be buried in the Cemetery.

After Sheffield, the family was based in Manchester, where Jane died of a cerebral hemorrhage while waiting to go on stage at the Free Trade Hall. She was 45. The Manchester Courier 15 February 1890 reported her death and included two sentences about her career, because, as a performer, she had a public profile. According to another newspaper report, she was "noted for her impersonation of Lady Macbeth". Jane's eldest child, Florence Livesey, married soon afterwards. Her youngest son Alfred, who was only seven when Jane died, emigrated to the US ten years later where he pursued a career as an actor.

Jane Callender is buried in the Nonconformist area, Section N, Plot 88, with her husband and daughter Edwina.

Maria Gomersal

In 1861, at the age of 17, Maria Gomersal, the daughter of a musician, was recorded in the census as being an actress, boarding with a family in Wrexham. Two years later she married William Gomersal, who was lessee of Theatre Royal from 1869 to 1872. In the 1871 census she was described as an operatic singer and actress, and Maria had already toured in the United States with great success. A review of a performance at the Theatre Royal which appeared in the *Sheffield Independent* 27 December 1869 was full of praise:

> Mrs Gomersal, who represents the hero of the pantomime, is an actress in whose hands the character receives full justice. Possessed of a charming voice, which she knows how to use to the best advantage, she sings the songs allotted to her in a manner which must have surprised those who had not previously heard her, and she plays in such an easy, graceful way that no wonder the hunchback becomes the ardent lover he does.............no audience would tire of hearing songs sung as she sings them.

She died at the tragically young age of 26, leaving a 6-year-old daughter. Her death was reported in the *Sheffield Daily Telegraph* 1 June 1871 and, as a performer, details were given of her career:

> ...Mrs Gomersal was the only daughter of the late Wm. Ribbon, musical composer. She was the first lady who played 'The Grand Duchess' in its English form, translated by her husband, and which was first produced in America at Mr Edwin Booth's Theatre, Philadelphia. As a lyric actress Mrs Gomersal had attained one of the most prominent positions in the United States. Her first appearance in opera was at the Boston Theatre, when she played Arline in 'The Bohemian Girl'. So great was her popularity and the desire to witness her debut, that the house was overcrowded in all parts, the receipts amounting to over sixteen hundred dollars. After visiting New York, she travelled with her husband through all the principal cities, and in August 1868, she returned to this country merely on a visit, but was never able to return...

The writer went on to suggest the cause of what became a two-year terminal illness: "...in consequence of a sudden illness produced from bathing at Margate, where, by inadvertently entering the water while in a state of perspiration, she laid the foundation of all her sufferings."

She is buried alone, to the side of Sandford Walk. The inscription to Maria reads: "In affectionate remembrance of Maria Gomersal, wife of William Gomersal, lessee of the Theatre Royal, Sheffield. She departed this life on the 9th day of June 1871 aged 26."

Sadly, there is no mention of her career, only that of her husband, her status in death depending on his.

Maria Gomersal was buried in the Anglican area, Section V1, Plot 157.

Jean Mitchell Saltfleet

Jean's father, Young Mitchell, was the first principal of Sheffield School of Art, which opened in 1843, and the man she married in 1904, Frank Saltfleet, was a well-known Sheffield artist and teacher. Jean, however, was an artist in her own right. She exhibited three times at the Royal Academy, and taught figure painting at Sheffield School of Art for 20 years before resigning to open her own studio in 1924. Jean was a

Miss Jean Mitchell.

noted portrait painter, painting the portraits of prominent Sheffield citizens among other subjects. Her sister Jessie was also an artist and exhibited at the Royal Academy in 1902.

Jean was buried in the Anglican area, Section H, Plot 107, with her husband and two sisters, Jessie and Florence Nightingale Mitchell.

Politically Engaged Women

Mary Holberry

Mary Holberry was born Mary Cooper in Attercliffe in 1816. Her father John was a labourer. In 1838, aged 22, Mary married Samuel Holberry. This was the year that the People's Charter was published, a text which became the foundation of a mass movement calling for widespread political reform, including the right of every man to have the vote, secret ballots, payment for MPs - so that ordinary men could stand for election - and annual parliaments. It was known as the Chartist movement.

Chartism quickly gathered support among working men and women and huge rallies were held nationwide. Many hundreds of thousands of people signed the Charter, which was presented to parliament. About one third of the signatories were women.

Samuel Holberry was one of the leaders of the Sheffield Chartists and Mary was an active supporter. He organised meetings at which he also spoke and famously was involved in an uprising in 1840, during which he and his companions planned to take over the town hall. The radicals were betrayed and both Samuel and Mary among those arrested. Mary, who was pregnant at the time, was kept in custody for two days and interrogated. She refused to cooperate and was released without charge. Samuel, however, was charged with sedition and sentenced to four years in prison. Mary petitioned in vain for his release, writing to newspapers and politicians. Samuel refused to allow her to visit him. He wrote: "My dear, you say you should like to come to York to see me; to that I cannot give my consent. In the first place we should have to look through the odious bars and it would only make you more unhappy…"

Mary's husband died aged 27 in 1842. He had been forced to work, illegally, on the treadmill which destroyed his already poor health.

Their son, Samuel John, was born in May 1840 but died 18 weeks later. He was buried in a public grave, B 47, in the Nonconformist area.

Mary remained active in the Chartist movement. In 1844 she joined them on a picket line in support of a miners' strike. She married again, to Charles Pearson, a publican, and went on to have more children, the first of whom she named Holberry Pearson. In 1845 she was described by a Chartist newspaper:

> After three years of heart corroding activity and mental anguish, she is still a truly fine woman, tall in stature, of graceful deportment, handsome expression and possesses an excellent temper and considering the defects of education, a mind of no mean order.

She is buried in the same grave as her first husband, as is her second husband and their first child, Holberry Pearson, but they are not memorialised on the headstone.

Mary died at the age of 67 in 1883 and is buried in the same grave as Samuel Holberry, in the Nonconformist area, Section G, Plot 55, a grave paid for by the Chartist Association.

Alice Hall

Alice Hall, nee Marples, was married with four children, the youngest only two years old, when her husband, Henry Foljambe Hall, died in 1905, aged 41. He had been managing director in the family firm of John Hall and Sons, Colonial Merchants, and Alice was left in comfortable circumstances. Unlike Queen Victoria who had withdrawn from public life after the death of Prince Albert, Alice Hall devoted her considerable talents to improving the world in which she lived.

She published three books of children's fairy tales, "The One Strand River and Other Fairy Tales" in 1903, "Godmother's

Stories" in 1912 and "The Cat, the Dog and the Dormouse" in the early 1920s. Her stories were charming but also modern for the

time. In "The Pirate Princess", for example, a princess decides she wants to become a pirate, and her father, having been persuaded, has a ship built for her while her mother insists she have the proper training. She lives happily ever after of course, but her prince is someone who ran away to be a sailor. Theirs is an equal partnership.

Actively involved on committees of the National Council of Women, and always interested in women's issues, Alice Hall's thoughtful, balanced letters on the subject of women's suffrage, written under the name CORNELIA, appeared in the *Sheffield Telegraph*. She campaigned for the appointment of women police officers. She also gave her time and expertise to Sheffield's The House of Help, founded, like the National Council for Women, in the last decade of the 19th century, and formed to support vulnerable girls and women, providing a temporary refuge and training for employment. The House of Help did not close its doors until 2005.

She was active in several other charitable organisations, including the Soldiers' and Sailors' Families' Association, founded in 1885, which became the Soldiers', Sailors and Airmens' Families' Association in 1919. Her children, as they grew up, put on dramatic events each Christmas to raise money for local charities. In 1924 she was appointed a J.P.

Alice died in 1935 and is buried with her husband and son to the right of the main gate on Cemetery Road. The monument was taken down in the 1980s, but the pink granite cross with its inscription is displayed on the incline next to the main drive, not far from the Gatehouse. Bequests were left to Sheffield Royal Hospital, Sheffield House of Help to Friendless Girls and to the Jessop Women's Hospital.

Alice Hall's life began in the Victorian era but reached forward to our own time in her visions for women. Not content merely to talk about the issues of the time, she worked tirelessly to improve the lot of all women and of society as a whole.

Alice Hall is buried in the Anglican area, Section E, Plot 82. The grave has been cleared but the cross is next to the main drive.

Eliza Rooke

In 1851 the first women's suffrage organisation in the country was founded in Sheffield, 50 years before the famous suffragette movement. Anne Knight, an Essex social reformer and pioneer of feminism, in correspondence with Isaac Ironside – a Sheffield Chartist and councillor, also buried in the Cemetery – asked if he could suggest women who would be interested in campaigning for female suffrage. He gave her a list of seven politically active women and Eliza Rooke was one of those women. Together Knight and these working-class Sheffield women formed the Sheffield Women's Political Association.

The first meeting was held on the 26th February 1851 at the Democratic Temperance Hotel, 33 Queen Street, Sheffield. The meeting unanimously adopted an "Address to the Women of England" which constitutes the first manifesto calling for female suffrage in Great Britain. The Sheffield Women's Political Association persuaded Lord Carlisle to submit this as a petition to the House of Lords, where it was roundly defeated.

Eliza was born in Brigg, Lincolnshire in 1824 and was married to Thomas Rooke, a confectioner. Thomas was a prominent Chartist – the two movements became strongly linked. Eliza was also a member of the National Chartist Association.

The Association lobbied widely, writing to newspapers, attending meetings throughout the country and encouraging other towns to form their own women's suffrage groups. The fame of the Association must have been considerable – in a commentary in the London Globe of March 1851 there is a disparaging reference to the "spirit of Sheffield gynaeocracy" and how it might affect a commission of inquiry into divorce law.

The life of the Association seems to have been short – there is no further mention of it in newspapers after 1853, but it was extremely significant in the development of the Suffrage movement.

Eliza died in 1856 aged 32 and is buried in a public grave, one of 19 burials in the same plot, including three children who died in the Sheffield flood of 1864.

Eliza Rooke is buried in the Anglican area, Section G2, Plot 126.

Women and Medicine

Kate Bolton and Emmeline Evans

Kate Bolton and Emmeline Evans exemplify the late Victorian professional woman. Their chosen career was nursing, one of the few careers open to women at that time.

There was no state registration for nurses until 1919, although since the work of Florence Nightingale it had been widely recognised that the need for trained nurses was critical. Various dignitaries and organisations set up schemes to train women for the profession, including the Queen Victoria Nursing Association, funded from the proceeds of Queen Victoria's Jubilee celebrations.

The Sheffield Nurses Home and Training Institution seems to have operated as a physical home for nurses, a training establishment, and as an agency where private clients could obtain a trained nurse to care for an invalid at home. It was established in 1871 and supported financially by many notable Sheffield businessmen.

Kate Bolton was a nurse at the Sheffield Nurses' Home. She died in October 1898 aged 27, as a result of an illness caught whilst at work. Her last posting had been at the Crimicar Lane Fever hospital.

Emmeline Evans was born in Camelford, Cornwall, the daughter of a Methodist minister. She trained with the Queen Victoria Nursing Association and in 1901 was working in a London cancer hospital, but by 1911 she was the Superintendent of the Sheffield Nurses Home and Training Institution. Her sister, Marion, had married a Sheffield man and this might be why she took up the post in Sheffield.

We also learn that Miss Evans was interested in the Anti-Suffrage League, though we cannot know from her attendance at this meeting to what extent she may have been involved. The Sheffield Daily Telegraph of Wednesday 9 June 1909, reports that a "drawing-room meeting of the Anti-Suffrage League was held at Ashdell Cottage, the residence of Mrs. J. Biggin". "Mrs. Laycock pleaded that women do not, as a class, desire the responsibility voting thrust upon them." She further pointed out in claiming votes for women, "that so vast a number of the voters would be young women who would exercise their votes only in days of youth and inexperience and comparative lack of interest in politics. They marry, on average at the age of 25, and then would lose the right to vote..."

Then in 1915, whilst attending a play at the Lyceum Theatre, Emmeline had a seizure and died aged 47 years. She was buried in the same grave as Kate Bolton. Their stone was moved to the wall bordering Cemetery Road after the Anglican area was cleared. The stone reads:

> In memory of Nurse Kate Bolton who died October 17, 1898, aged 27 years. He hath done all things well.

> Also Emmeline Evans, Lady Superintendent of the Sheffield Nurse's Home born 6 Oct 1868 - died 15 Dec 1915.

Emmeline left £361 to her sister.

Kate Bolton was buried in the cleared Anglican area, Section H1 Plot 65, a grave purchased for her by the Nurses Home. Emmeline Evans is buried in the same plot. The headstone from the grave has been moved to the wall bordering Cemetery Road.

Attracta Genevieve Rewcastle

Attracta Genevieve Candon, known as Eva, was born in Roscommon, Ireland in 1897. Her father was a publican and farmer and moderately well off as the family employed two servants. Eva, and one of her sisters, went to the National University of Ireland in Dublin to study medicine.

Eva qualified in 1921 and moved to Sheffield where she became an Assistant Schools' Medical Officer. It could be that it was here that she met her future husband, Cuthbert Snowball Rewcastle. He was a barrister who stood as the Liberal Party candidate for the Sheffield Hallam constituency in the General Elections of 1922 and 1923. Her parents moved to Sheffield from Ireland at about that time. Eva and Cuthbert were married in 1926 and Eve began work at the Great Ormond Street Hospital in London. She was very active in the Catholic Women's League and was awarded a Papal gold medal for this service. From 1931 to 1939, in addition to having three children and continuing her work at Great Ormond Street, Eva continued in private practise in London. In 1939  she was commissioned in the Royal Naval Volunteer Reserve and thus became the first woman doctor to be appointed to the Royal Navy. Her appointment caused some controversy as officers in the Women's Royal Naval Service (Wrens) were paid less than their male counterparts in the navy. Outside the armed forces, female doctors were paid the same as male doctors, and the Medical Women's Federation objected to Eva being paid less that a man in a similar position. As a result, she was promoted to the rank of Surgeon Lieutenant-Commander. As well as blazing a trail for aspiring female officers, Eva secured the appointment of 20 female Surgeon Lieutenants to the RNVR where previously there had been none. She was awarded an OBE in 1946 in recognition of her wartime service.

After the war Eve returned to the Great Ormond Street hospital and worked as a maternity and child welfare officer in South London. She was Chairman of the National Board of Catholic Women from 1945 until 1947 and became a Conservative Councillor on Westminster City Council. She also stood as a Conservative parliamentary candidate in the 1950 election but was defeated. She was then selected to run for the more 'winnable' seat of Coventry in the next election but died of oesophageal cancer in 1951.

Two months after she died, her son Anthony – who was in the Royal Navy – died in a tragic submarine accident. Her daughter, Rosalind, became a prominent microbiologist.

Attracta Genevieve Rewcastle is buried with her parents and sister in the Anglican area, Section E, Plot 32. The memorial stone has been lost.

Ethel Close Turner

Ethel Close was born in 1882 in Bradford, the daughter of a baker. In 1911 Ethel was a trained nurse, working at the Seacroft Hospital in Leeds. We know from that she served in France as a nurse in the First World War and also worked at the Military Fever Hospital in Scarborough, from the memorial inscription:

> In loving memory of Ethel Close, beloved wife of Rev. George Turner, who served her country in France, was matron of the military fever hospital in Scarborough, during the Great War,

beloved medical missionary to the Cree Indians, N.W. Canada, died Dec. 21st, 1934, aged 52 years.

It is unusual to find an inscription to a woman which is so detailed. Attitudes had changed significantly by the 1930s, but even Alice Hall, who did so much to help women's causes and who ended her career as a JP, and died in 1936, was described merely as 'the beloved wife' of Henry, who had died thirty years previously.

Perhaps it was while she was nursing that she met her future husband, George Turner. He was born in Leeds and trained there at the Headingly College as a Minister. His war service was spent in Canada, serving in the Canadian Expeditionary Force.

Ethel and George were married in Alberta, Canada. George was appointed as the Principal of a Canadian School and a missionary to the Cree Indians. These schools are now seen as very controversial. Children were separated from their families and their culture, and the regime was harsh.

In 1923 George became the vicar of St Margaret's Church, Limerick, Canada. The parish totalled 1,600 acres territory. Ethel is described as a 'medical missionary', obviously using her nursing skills to care for the local population. Ethel's health was not good, and the couple returned to England where George became Curate in Darfield, Barnsley. He was then appointed, in 1929, as Vicar of St Jude's in Moorfields Sheffield. This was considered an extremely poor parish, and Ethel's nursing abilities were again put to good use.

George died in January 1930 aged 56 years. He left a small estate of £408 to Ethel. She died two years later aged 52 years.

Ethel Turner is buried with her husband in the cleared Anglican area, Section D, Plot 67.

Women of Means

Martha Bragge

Born in Essex in 1816, Martha was the child of Martha and James Beddow, a druggist, both staunch Congregationalists. She had two brothers: George, who studied medicine before training as an Anglican minister, and dying in Australia at the age of 41, and Benjamin, who became a congregationalist minister in Barnsley. Martha herself worked as a governess to the Beaumont family in Birmingham. There she met her husband William Bragge, an engineer and surveyor. Their first child, Martha Jane, known as Jennie, was born in Chester where William worked as a "locomotive manager" for the Chester and Birkenhead Railway. Two years later their son Charles William, or Charlie, was born, and the following year William was offered work in Brazil to build a gas works and railway, which he accepted. Martha and the family joined him in the spring of 1852, and apart from a brief return in England in 1855, the family remained in South America until 1857.

Martha wrote regularly to her mother while they were abroad, as well as to William when work commitments took him away. Some of those letters, perhaps only a small percentage, were kept and donated to Sheffield Archives by Jennie in old age. They reveal someone who was in many ways the ideal of a Victorian middle-class wife – deferring to her husband, managing home and servants, caring and dutiful – but who was also an independent thinker.

Despite William's important and well-paid work (he received a medal from Emperor Dom Pedro II in appreciation of his work in Brazil), Martha's life in South America was not easy. The letters to her mother from Rio de Janeiro and later from Buenos Aires are frequently hurried, full of love to be given to relations and friends, and assurances about everyone's health. She had to contend with the difficulties of language, extreme heat, and "vermin of all kinds." Martha could rely on her husband's large income, but expense was always on her mind – the expense of servants, the expense of paying the passage of a governess to come out from England (and sometimes to be sent back), the expense of the seasonal moves. As a family they moved from one house to another to escape the city in the hot season, with Martha packing and unpacking for an entire household. Two of her children were born while they were away, George in Rio de Janeiro, and Anne in Buenos Aires. Boxes had to be sent out with supplies of everything from England, particularly when they were in Rio – replacement cutlery, items of clothing, linen with which to make baby clothes. Health was always an anxiety; references are made to fever and the possibility of smallpox. Medical help was rudimentary; Martha relied on a recipe for the treatment of worms from an acquaintance and used poultices for the boils which seemed to plague everyone occasionally. The children were dosed with cod liver oil. Another remedy for ill health was to send the children or herself to stay with friends in the country for a rest and change of air. In 1853 a boil on her upper lip was treated "3 times with caustic and twice it was lanced, not deftly, and now I have a hole and a scar by no means adding to any beauty"; her doctor advised her "to drink porter and port wine and to eat chops – all expensive articles!" The birth of George was without incident but before long she was suffering from mastitis and in agony. Eventually she was forced to give up breast feeding, and a wet nurse was engaged.

Letters to William during his frequent absences were concerned with practicalities, and gave news of the children, but she hated the separations and, frustrated by constant delays in the post, expressed her longing to see him, her depression and loneliness, while assuring him she did not let this show to the "Dots" as she referred to the children.

There is a sense in the letters to her mother that much is not said – saved for when they can speak face to face. Accustomed to managing servants in England, she was shocked and depressed by the injustice of the system in Brazil: "I intend when I have more time, to make a few comments on slavery but not this time. Your remarks are indeed to a great extent true as to man being vile" (1852) and later: "There is now some movement to try to put matters on a better footing – what the result will be I can't tell. It is a cold heartless affair altogether, and how to improve things is a most difficult question."

Martha's Black servants seemed to be hired out to them from local landowners; their wages were paid to their master. Martha formed a bond with a servant, Ignacia, which was strengthened during her struggles after Georgie's birth:

> My faithful Ignacia was a teacher (?) to me, so kind, patient and thoughtful, …. in encouraging me and her sympathy with my endurance

> But Ignacia was pregnant, and Martha was afraid that her master "will claim the child and let her out as wet nurse at high wages. This is Slavery!" She noted that Ignacia was married but not with her husband. "This is often the case and is a matter of course here. I don't pretend to justify these things – I only tell them as facts and beyond my control."

When Ignacia had to leave, she writes: "I miss her every moment of the day, and find how valuable a servant she is. I really love Ignacia. The parting was quite affecting, [she] cried over me... I cried too and often could cry now from want of her." And adds, "I am quietly making observations on all these things ... - many things here that seem strange at first I am satisfied must be changed most gradually..." (By 1852 slaves were no longer being brought into Brazil, but slavery was not abolished there until 1888.)

She was at first much happier in Buenos Aries. It was easier to buy necessities and she felt that as a place to live was "nicer in every respect," but gradually she became disillusioned with the gossip and difficulties inherent in a small community. With the completion of William's work, they returned to England, to Sheffield, and William became a partner in John Brown and Company. At first, they lived in Collegiate Crescent and then moved into Shirle Hill, Cherry Tree Road. Their adventures abroad were not entirely over because William travelled of behalf of the firm and Martha sometimes went with him.

Sadly, in the 1870s, Martha's health began to deteriorate and despite several stays at Buxton Spa, she died in 1877 aged 59, of "anaemia of the brain" and "atrophy of the brain". Mrs Beddow had died in 1865. William arranged for his wife to be buried with her mother, gave up all his public positions in Sheffield, sold his house, auctioned the contents, and moved back to Birmingham where he died seven years later.

Curiously, the inscription on the headstone reads:

> In affectionate remembrance of Grandmama Beddow who departed this life October 24th 1865 aged 88 years.
>
> And of Martha, only daughter of the above Martha Beddow, wife of Alderman William Bragge FSA of Shirle Hill, Sheffield, born 31st October 1818, died 30th March 1877.

Who decided to describe Martha Beddow 'Grandma Beddow'? Her daughter – sometimes her begins her letters 'Dear Grandma' – or a grandchild?

Martha Bragge and Martha Beddow are buried in the Nonconformist area, Section EE, plot 66, below the Nonconformist Chapel, now known as the Samuel Worth Chapel.

Alice Roberts

Alice Roberts died in 1926, two years before the Equal Franchise act gave voting rights to women as well as men. She was 82 years old, the widow of Thomas Roberts, founder of Messrs T. and J. Roberts, one of Sheffield's best known department stores, and the mother of three sons and two daughters. She lived at 1 Kenwood Bank, a villa which was built for her by the Roberts family between 1899 and 1900. Alice had been a tireless worker with the East Circuit of the Wesleyan Methodist Chapel, Moorfoot, for over sixty years, and held both the office of President of the Brunswick Ladies' Circuit and of the Foreign Society. The Wesleyan Methodists were the oldest and largest of Sheffield's Methodist bodies. Brunswick Chapel was opened in 1834 and stood near the traffic lights at St Mary's Gate. It was  demolished in the 1950s to make way for Sheffield's inner ring road. Six hundred persons had been buried in the Chapel Burial Ground which was lost to a previous road widening scheme; their remains were re-interred in the cemetery catacombs in 1933. An article in the *Sheffield Daily Independent* Saturday 26 May 1934 which celebrates the Chapel's Centenary, also notes "last year considerable interest was taken in the removal of the old graveyard in front of the Chapel. This became necessary for widening the road to build 4 shops…which will be opened shortly".

Alice is buried to the side of the Anglican Chapel. As well as being memorialised on the family monument, Alice has an additional memorial stone set at ground level and inscribed:

In loving memory of Aunt Roberts, whose kindness and hospitality to them during the Great War, will always be gratefully remembered by her Australian nephews.

It is believed that Mrs Roberts opened her home to convalescing ANZAC soldiers during the First World War, so it seems likely that the 'Australian nephews' who commemorated her 'kindness and hospitality' were Australian soldiers.

Alice Roberts was buried with other family members in the Anglican area, Section E, Plot 168/9.

Nancy Senior

While the deaths of many nineteenth century businessmen were reported in the local newspapers, with obituaries written and funerals described in detail, their wives' deaths, no matter how much they contributed to their husbands' success, were only noted briefly in the Births, Marriages and Deaths column. Victorian wives, traditionally seen as the guardians of the house and hearth, remained in the background, hidden behind their husbands' names. The earliest report of a prominent woman's funeral in the cemetery that has been found to date, is that of Mrs George Senior, who died in 1913, twelve years after the death of Queen Victoria. The Senior family monument is one of those which survived the council clearance and can be seen to the left of the path which runs parallel to Cemetery Road, a short distance from the Anglican Chapel.

Mrs George Senior, born in 1839 in Bradfield, was Nancy Parkin, the daughter of Edwin Parkin, an iron forge man. When she was 20, she married George Senior, a steel forgeman, just out of his apprenticeship and a few months older. They began their lives together, as George stated bluntly, "with nothing." Nancy could surely never have imagined that the working man she had married would become a notable steel manufacturer at first, then Lord Mayor, and finally Master Cutler, with the result that she would be expected to take on the public roles and social responsibilities of Lady Mayoress and Mistress Cutler.

The young couple moved to Sheffield and were living in Neepsend at the time of the Sheffield Flood. Their house was directly in the path of the water, but they escaped with their baby, before George returned to help others. Even when George acquired the tenancy of Pond's Forge, they faced difficult times before achieving ownership and financial security. The *Sheffield Telegraph*, reporting on her life and funeral, noted that George "was always ready to acknowledge the help he had from [his wife] during this period." And continued:

> Mrs. Senior was ever warm-hearted and generous, and in the days of prosperity, which came as business at the Ponds Forge grew, she was able in a quiet and unostentatious way to help many of those who were not so happily situated, financially, as she was. Of a retiring disposition, Mrs. Senior preferred the quiet and comfort of her own home to the busy round of society appointments. But notwithstanding this she made an excellent Lady Mayoress and Mistress Cutler.

Mrs Senior supported the Sunday School of the Blind Institution in West Street, and "her kindly disposition endeared her to all with whom she came in contact, both in society circles and in humbler walks of life." While Lady Mayoress she "gave a dinner to the adult blind of the city, and later, at the Botanical Gardens, she entertained all the children from the workhouses, orphanages, and other charitable institutions in the city."

Only three years before her sudden death in 1913, the couple had celebrated their 50th wedding anniversary. Mr. and Mrs. Senior entertained the workpeople at Ponds Forge in celebration of their golden wedding, and later at their own home there was a family gathering which was attended by all their grownup children and their thirteen grandchildren.

Regrets for her death and sympathy for her husband's loss were expressed by people from all walks of life. The Duke of Norfolk sent a telegram telling of his "deep regret and grief" and more than two hundred of her husband's employees walked in procession from Elmfield, the Senior home in Broomhill, to Carver Street Wesleyan Chapel for the first part of the service and afterwards to the Cemetery.

Nancy is buried with her husband and other family members in the Anglican area, Section G1, Plot 7.

Catherine Parker

On 4th May 1844 when she was 54 years old, Catherine Parker took her own life with her son's razor at her home 6 Broomhall Place.

In 1792, two years after Catherine's birth, Mary Wollstonecraft wrote the influential work "Vindication of the Rights of Women", but the first Married Women's Property Act wasn't introduced until 1870, and during Catherine's married life women belonged to their husbands. Wives had no legal rights, they could not own property, earn their own money or keep it, and they could not be guardians of their own children.

However, Catherine's husband, William, died suddenly, intestate, in 1837, "in a fit of apoplexy", so Catherine shouldered the burden of winding up the family business as well as carrying out her traditional family responsibilities which included overseeing the prospects of five children. According to the report of the inquest in the Sheffield Independent 11th May 1844, she had "immense anxieties and much to manage". The affecting details of her deteriorating condition perhaps indicate the symptoms of a depressive illness.

"Self-murder" became a crime under common law in the thirteenth century, and as late as 1958 a man was prosecuted and sent to prison for attempting suicide. In 1823 the Burial of Suicides Act allowed burials of those who took their own lives to take place in consecrated ground, but without a religious service. The body had to be buried privately between 9 pm and midnight. This law was amended in 1882 and suicide burials could take place at any time, but still without full church rites, and although the Suicide Act of 1961 decriminalised suicide, it wasn't until 2015 that the Church of England Synod allowed full Anglican burial rites. In 1844, for a family member to be the subject of an inquest in this way would have been not only shocking and painful, but also socially embarrassing. Perhaps this is why Catherine was buried alone near the Choragic monument which commemorates her husband. William Parker and other family members are buried to the side of the Nonconformist (or Samuel Worth) Chapel. Catherine is memorialised on the family stone with everyone else.

Catherine Parker is buried in the Nonconformist area, Section Z, Plot 173. Her husband and family are buried in the Nonconformist area, Vault T 8.

Ulrith, Amelia and Maria Shore

Buried in HH 115 in the Nonconformist area are three of the daughters of Samuel Shore of Norton. Samuel came from a Sheffield family of bankers and tradesmen and married Urith Offley, who inherited Norton Hall. The family was wealthy and moved in the highest circles – Lady Urith Shore was painted by George Romney, the most celebrated portrait artist of his day.

Samuel and Urith had six daughters and two sons. There is a famous story often told in Sheffield history books of an incident when King George III was taking a walk on Weymouth beach. He saw some children playing with their nurse and asked who the children were. He was told that they were Mr Shore's children, of Norton, Sheffield. "Sheffield! Sheffield! Damn bad place, Sheffield" the King is reported to have remarked! These children were also related to Florence Nightingale – her father was a Shore who changed his name to Nightingale to benefit from an inheritance – and the cousins used to play together when they were young.

Three of the daughters, Urith Lydia, Amelia Theophila and Maria Theodosia remained unmarried and lived together at Meersbrook. In the 1851 Census Urith is described as a 'Landed proprietor'. The three women had five servants to look after them. When Samuel died, he was buried in the graveyard of Norton Church, in spite of being a prominent non-conformist. However, when his daughter Maria Amelia died in 1855 the vicar of Norton was away, and the Curate refused to buy her in the churchyard as she was not of the Anglican faith. Urith bought a grave at the Sheffield General Cemetery and Maria was laid to rest

there. The idea of a Shore being shut out of Norton Church created much angry feeling and there were letters to the newspaper, condemning the "churlish priest":

The old Sheffield family of Shore, long known to entertain Unitarian sentiments, has been settled in the parish of Norton for generations. Its past members, and in an eminent degree its present members, have been the general benefactors of the neighbourhood. For more than a century Norton Church has been the family burial place. The present members of the family have been on the most friendly and neighbourly terms with the Vicar of Norton, the Rev. H. H. Pearson, as well as with his father, the late Vicar, whom he succeeded. The death of Miss Maria Theodosia Shore, of Meersbrook, youngest daughter of the late Samuel Shore, Esq., was announced in our last, and the family proposed that her interment should take place, according to their custom, at Norton Church. But strange to say, the Rev. Mr. Sale, the curate of the parish, gave them to understand that he should refuse to read the funeral service over the deceased, because she was a Unitarian. The Vicar was from home at the time, but it is understood that he adopted, and sanctioned by letter, the conduct of his curate. The result has been that Miss M. T. Shore is interred at the Sheffield Cemetery. Thus do the Shores, from no change in themselves, but from a new reading of church law, or at least from a new practice, find that they are deprived of their ancient burying place; and clergymen, with whom they have been on most friendly terms in life, pronounce them in death to be unfit for Christian burial.

From the *Sheffield Independent* of 29 September 1855.

Maria Theodosia Shore is buried with Urith and Amelia in the Nonconformist area, Section HH, Plot 115. Only Maria's name is recorded on the monument.

Amy Cripps Vernon

In 1900, at the age of 30, Amy Cripps Vernon found herself a widow with two sons under the age of four. She was one of nine grownup children of Thomas Young, a minister of the Catholic Apostolic Church, and when her husband, a minister of the same church, died leaving only £205, she left Wolverhampton, where they were living, and returned to Sheffield to live in the family home with her sons, then aged three and one. In 1901 the family home was shared with her parents, five grown up siblings, and a servant. Amy had begun writing stories for younger children in 1896; her last was published in 1915. Many of her stories were published by the Christian Knowledge Society (later the Society for Promoting Christian Knowledge.) Her stories also appeared in The Irish Times. She died in 1956.

Amy Cripps Vernon is buried in the cleared Anglican area, Section E1, Plot 56, with her parents and two grown up sons.

Index of Names

Andrews, Mary   p.33

Barber, Harriet and Mary Ann   p.33

Bell, Mary   p.19

Bennett, Olivia   p.42

Binns, Jemima   p.35

Blagdon, Elizabeth   p.18

Bolton, Kate   p.60

Bragge, Martha   p.65

Burr, Annie Elizabeth   p.37

Cadman, Hannah and Mary   p.8, 38

Callender, Jane   p.8, 51

Cheshire, Sarah   p.18

Clarborough, Martha   p.32

Clarke, Minnie   p.19

Cowlishaw, Sarah   p.32

Evans, Emmeline   p.60

Fawcett, Mary, Marianne and Martha   p.39

Firth, Elizabeth   p.21

Fish, Mary Ann   p.10

Gill, Elizabeth   p.43

Gomersal, Maria   p.8, 52

Grace, Sarah   p.11, 23

Green, Margaret   p.29

Guest, Evangeline Lothian   p.23

Hall, Alice   p.7, 56

Holberry, Mary   p.55

Howgate, Ann   p.31

Jacques, Phoebe   p.19

Lindley, Louise   p.31

Marshall, Jane   p.11

May, Emma   p.44

Meeson, Ada   p.25

Nield, Elizabeth   p.11, 27

Oates, Louisa   p.46

Parker, Catherine   p.7, 12, 73

Parkin, Ann   p.28

Rewcastle, Attracta Genevieve   p.62

Roberts, Catherine   p.19

Roberts, Alice   p.69

Rooke, Eliza   p.58

Rose, Jane   p.19

Rudd, Frances Mary   p.47

Saltfleet, Jean Mitchell   p.54

Scattergood, Mary   p.48

Senior, Nancy   p.8, 71

Shore, Ulrith, Amelia and Maria   p.74

Snape, Mary   p.40

Taylor, Charlotte   P.8, .41

Turner, Ethel Close   p.63

Vernon, Amy Cripps   p.77

Whewell, Mary Ann   p.10

Wilkin, Mary Ann   p.50

Sources:

Sheffield General Cemetery Trust Archives

Sheffield City Archives and Local Studies Library

Tweedale's Directory of Sheffield Cutlery Manufacturers 1740-2013 Revised and Expanded 2nd Edition Geoffrey Tweedale 2019

Census records 1841 – 1911

National Probate Calendar

Women Workers in Sheffield's Metal Trades c. 1742 – 1867 Laura R. Bracey 2016
https://etheses.whiterose.ac.uk/16536/1/Laura%20Roisin%20Bracey%20Thesis.pdf

https://sheffielder.net/tag/jean-saltfleet/

National Farmers Union. World War 1: The Few that Fed the Many https://www.nfuonline.com/archive?treeid=33538

https://www.undercliffecemetery.co.uk/

https://arnosvale.org.uk/

Picture Credits:

Picture Sheffield (Sheffield Archives & Local Studies Library), pages 40, 43, 54, 65, 71, 75

Hawley Tool Collection, Kelham Island Museum, page 34

Geoffrey Tweedale, page 38

Wikipedia, pages 45, 62

SGCT Archives, pages 10, 29, 35, 75

Janna Williams, family photo of Alice Hall, page 57

Shirley Baxter, pages 16, 31, 47, 50, 51, 60, 70

Charles Lees, Frontispiece and pages 13, 14, 15, 16, 17

Carole Burgess, page 71

Further Reading:

Sweet Remembrance, Andrew Littlewood, edited by Sue Turner (2023) Sheffield General Cemetery Trust

Remote and Undisturbed, A brief history of Sheffield General Cemetery by Jane Horton. Revised edition Jo Meredith (2014) Sheffield General Cemetery Trust

Made in Sheffield, Victorian Cutlers and Metal Workers by Shirley Baxter and Jean Lees (2022) Sheffield General Cemetery Trust

Martha Bragge letters, Sheffield Archives

Sheffield General
Cemetery Trust

First opened in 1836, the Cemetery was the final resting place for 87,000 people before closing for burials in 1978.

The Cemetery, now a Listed Grade II* Historic Landscape, lay abandoned and overgrown for many years but has been carefully restored by Sheffield City Council and the Sheffield General Cemetery Trust. The many fine buildings, Victorian monuments and headstones now sit in a delightful parkland landscape of wildflowers and shady trees. The Cemetery Park is a recognised Local Nature Reserve, and its winding paths lead you past some of Sheffield's famous residents, from steel barons to radical chartists.

The Sheffield General Cemetery Trust is a charitable trust which with its committed volunteers maintains and develops the historic landscape and researches the history of the site and people buried there. For over 30 years the Trust has organised events and led tours of the site for the public, schools and community groups. The Trust restored its buildings, and the beautiful Samuel Worth Chapel is now available for events hire.

Visit our website **www.gencem.org** to find out more about the Cemetery.

"A Woman's Place" is one of a series of books created by volunteers of the Sheffield General Cemetery Trust which can be purchased through our website at **www.gencem.org**

Remote and Undisturbed
An illustrated history of the General Cemetery. From its beginnings in 1836 to provide much needed burial space for a rapidly growing city, through to the present day.

Price £7.95

A Window into the Workhouse
A detailed and moving insight into the lives of some of the people buried in the General Cemetery whose last residence was recorded as the workhouse, and the living and working conditions and attitudes to the poor in the nineteenth and early twentieth centuries.

Price £7.99

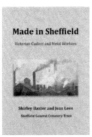

Made in Sheffield
A captivating book about more than 50 people linked to the metal and cutlery industries: their families, inventions, philanthropy, business failures and successes.

Price £7.99

Danger and Despair
A fascinating picture of Victorian life through the vivid descriptions of untimely death. Drawn from the Cemetery's burial records, these are tales of tragic accidents, rejected love, deep despair, and sometimes plain foolishness.

Price £7.95